How to Stop Being Manipulative

Step-by-Step Guide on How to Stop Being Manipulative, Stop Gas Lighting and How to Stop Being Overbearing to Have Healthy, Mutually-Beneficial Relationships

D1523275

Introduction

There are a ton of prospective reasons why you sought out this book.

It could be that your partner just told you, "Honey, you're a great person, but you're so manipulative that it sours just about everything else," or something along those lines.

It could be that your work colleagues have frequently mentioned how you'd be so much more fun to be around if you weren't so coercive.

It could be that you've lost a couple of friends whom you genuinely liked and loved being around, all because you did some things that they considered "manipulative and disrespectful." It could even be that you've had successive issues with members of their family for what they term as emotional abuse on your part.

Regardless of the reasons that drive you into picking up this book, it will answer every question you may have about being manipulative, detail what manipulative behavior entails, and show you how to break free from it if you are indeed manipulative.

If you discover that you are manipulative, understand that this does not necessarily make you a bad person. The mere fact that you had the sense and humility to seek this content and understand yourself better disqualifies you from being a bad person by default.

While that may be the case, if you are manipulative towards your friends and loved ones, understand that you have a lot of work to do, and if you are as committed to change as I believe you are, you have to commit to taking action on what you learn from this book. If for nothing else, at the end of it all, you (along with your loved ones) will be glad you made the necessary effort to improve.

With that out of the way, let's dive into it:

PS: I'd like your feedback. If you are happy with this book, please leave a review on Amazon.

Please leave a review for this book on Amazon by visiting the page below:

https://amzn.to/2VMR5qr

Table of Content

Part 1

Recognizing Manipulative Behavior

Chapter 1: What Exactly is Manipulation?

Because manipulative behavior is the essence of this book, the very first thing we must do is define what manipulation is by asking ourselves, *"what is manipulation?"*Perhaps the best way to define and understand manipulation is to describe what a manipulator is and what he or she does:

As a manipulator, you will get what you want via duplicitous and deceptive means. You are a 'black hat' operator who, rather than use moral, upstanding persuasion methods, will resort to underhanded tactics like threats, lies, and influence (the capacity to cause something without necessarily directing the action.) You will do all you can to change other people's minds or indirectly alter their actions.

Manipulators don't necessarily care about others. First and foremost, you will care about getting others to do what you want. Everything else comes second. Normal people, at least on some level, understand that they cannot always get their way. As, Chepe, one of the principal characters in the hit TV show, Narcos, alludes, *"a big part of being an adult is at times accepting things you don't necessarily want to accept and making the requisite adjustments."*

As a manipulator, you will often not think this way; you will not really understand this. If you can't get what you want straight up, you'll coerce, lie, badger, and use passive-aggressive tactics until you have your way. You will make the emotional atmosphere as toxic as you need to make it as long as you arrive at your wants. It's quite selfish when you look at it this way, no?

Quite obviously, manipulators are bad news. Nobody wants them in their lives—you do not want them in your life. A manipulator can easily lead you to compromise your morals and partake in behavior and activities that cause great discomfort.

However, what if you are a manipulative individual?

Unfortunately, most manipulators do not always know that they are manipulative. You may unconsciously exhibit manipulative behavior as you go about your daily life and interact with others.

At first, this may sound ridiculous; after all, how can anyone use toxic and manipulative behavior without knowing that they are indeed doing so? In truth, manipulation is just like any other kind of communication.

Everyone develops conversation strategies from a very young age based on what is effective and works for them. If manipulative communication strategies frequently get results, it usually follows that the person will keep using them.

The very first step in changing manipulative behavior is recognizing it. Look back at your life and your interaction with others, especially those closest to you and the people you love.

When they turn you down and say "no," do you accept it gracefully, or do you undercut their psyches until they thaw and give in? Do you use passive-aggressive behavior to cause other people so much discomfort so that they are less inclined to turn you down in the future? Have you ever thrown a hissy fit because you did not get your way?

Passive-aggressive behavior involves using underhanded emotional tactics like stonewalling, ignoring people, and answering them with curt, rude replies. It also involves deliberately making other people uneasy and uncomfortable, and overall, unbalancing their emotional makeup as much as you can to get your way.

The chapters in this section of the book, starting with the next chapter, will help you recognize manipulative behavior in your life and your day-to-day interactions.

Before we move on to that, it is important to highlight two behaviors closely related to manipulative behavior: *gaslighting* and *overbearingness*. The truth is that a significant percentage of manipulative persons practice one or both of these behaviors.

Let us shed some light on both, starting with gaslighting:

Gaslighting

Gaslighting is a type of psychological abuse where you make someone else question their sanity, perception of reality, and even their memories. When you gaslight a person, they will feel anxious, confused, and unable to trust themselves.

The term comes from the 1938 play Gaslight, later adapted to a movie in 1944. In the movie, the husband usually manipulates the spouse into believing she is having hallucinations and hence having a mental illness when what he's doing is dimming their gas-fueled lights.

Gaslighting will often develop gradually, which may make it difficult to detect. Here are some techniques you may be using to gaslight others; knowing these will allow you to know whether you use this manipulative behavior:

- **Countering:** Here, you will question another person's memories. You may say things like, "you never recall anything accurately," or 'are you really sure? Your memory is horrendous."

- **Withholding:** Here, you will refuse to engage in conversations. You may even pretend not to comprehend the subject matter so that you do not have to respond to the other person. For instance, you may say, "well, I do not know what you're talking about."

- **Trivializing:** Here, you will disparage or even outrightly disregard the other person's feelings. You may accuse the person of extreme sensitivity or "proneness to overreacting" when their concerns and feelings are valid.

- **Denial:** This one involves pretending to forget events or how they happened. You may deny saying something you said or accuse the other person of fictionalizing accounts, even when you know they're real.

Gaslighting is a commonly used tool in the manipulator's toolbox, as is the behavior we'll cover next: being overbearing.

Overbearingness

"Overbearing" typically describes someone who is haughty and dictatorial, which is something most manipulators are. Being overbearing means being domineering. For instance, if you have an overbearing instructor who criticizes every misstep you make, you may struggle to learn how to play the violin.

It may be tough to tell the difference between genuine assertiveness and (too) pushy habits because both have the end goal of helping you get what you want: having things work out as you want them to and telling people what you really think.

However, while assertiveness is an amazing skill to develop and something you should use regularly, pushiness is manipulative and will end up holding you back. Perhaps the best way to explain overbearing behavior is this:

Assertiveness is about expressing your needs directly and openly while maintaining respect for the other party's preferences and needs. On the other hand, overbearingness is about the belief that only your needs count. Thus, you push the other person's preferences and needs to the side to meet your, which boils down to manipulation.

With all this covered, let us look more closely at manipulative behaviors:

Chapter 2: Am I a Manipulative Person Without Knowing It?

Just about everyone has fallen subject to manipulative tactics at some point or other. However, nobody wants to view themselves as manipulative or admit to being so. Nevertheless, some manipulative behaviors are so common that you could be indulging in emotional coercion on the regular without even realizing that you are.

Manipulative behavior, according to New York-based psychotherapy expert Rebecca Hendrix, LMFT, ultimately comes down to *"conveying information in an indirect, roundabout manner."*

That may take various forms: from passive-aggressive, silent treatment—which we highlighted in the previous chapter, but boils down to ignorance, stonewalling, giving curt answers, and withholding affection, sex, etc.—to less blatant, more subtle actions like pretending to be the wounded individual or playing the martyr role, where you pretend to carry everyone's water and be the sacrificial lamb.

It entails persuading a person to do or to think something without explicitly addressing the issue. Hendrix explains,

"It's purposeful and strategic." "It's prioritizing my requirements over the other person's."

Here are some manipulative habits you may be guilty of and better ways to navigate the situation to bolster the health and longevity of your relationships.

#: Um, wouldn't you fancy...?

Hendrix cites "innocent" suggestion as an illustration of manipulative conduct. Innocent suggestions are when someone proposes something instead of just straight-up stating what they are thinking or feeling.

For example, if you're driving to a buddy's house and text them, "Do you fancy some beer after dinner? I'll grab a six-pack," when you know that your pal isn't a huge beer fan. You could go for a beer or two before going to your buddy's place or get your bottle after leaving their place, but no. Instead, you plant your suggestion in your friend's head and make it appear like the idea is theirs.

In essence, the element at play here is phrasing your desire in a way that makes it seem like the other person's. In reality, a better approach would be to phrase your desire more authentically. For example, in this case, you could say, "I believe I want a beer after dinner; would you fancy some?"

#: *It's completely up to you, but...*

Similarly, you could present a person with a choice when the truth is you've already decided for them. An example of this is asking a friend which of two movies they'd prefer to see, then outlining in detail why one is superior, all while maintaining that it is up to them to make a decision. For instance, you could say, "I'm 100% open to seeing the other one—but this movie is far more historical, and we will surely learn way more."

It's a little coercive to portray something as a choice when you're trying to force someone to choose one alternative over another. In contrast, "I prefer to watch this one. What says you?" is a more straightforward way to pose the same question.

#: *Oh, I forgot (again and again)*

If you have ever "forgotten" to perform a shared task like, say, a household chore because you were exhausted, it was late, or you just weren't up to it, rest assured: you are not alone.

However, if you've made a habit of saddling your partner or roommate with the dirty dishes or leaving your classmates or workmates to pick up your slack with projects, you might want to look deeply in the mirror.

Constantly failing to play your role in things and activities that affect everyone is downright unfair. If you are genuinely too swamped or tired, then you need to talk about it. It is always better to communicate honestly about what needs completing and actively find ways to handle the situation.

#: Promises and more promises

Overpromising is yet another habit used by manipulative people. This behavior might take the form of exaggerating the importance of an event or activity that you want a friend to attend or be part of—"It'll be amazing!". There're rumors that Elon Musk is on the guestlist!"—or making a promise but not following through—"I'll prepare lunch every day without fail next week!".

When you fail to keep your part of the bargain after you've raised the stakes, the other person may be dissatisfied, furious, and may even feel misled—and be rightfully disgruntled.

It's always best to be forthright. If your friend or partner does not want to participate in an activity you think is important, investigate the situation honestly and in a level-headed manner. Rather than strong-arm people into doing what you want, ask why and genuinely try to view things from their perspective.

#: *It's no big deal; I'll just do it myself...*

This one is a favorite of manipulative people. Casting yourself in the role of a martyr is a tactic that many people often use to get other people to do your bidding, albeit in a toxic, unhealthy way.

When you pressure somebody into doing something in a sneaky, indirect manner that is likely to induce feelings of guilt, you are being manipulative and using an ineffective way of asking for aid. For example, it's manipulative to say something like, "if you do not do this, then a bad thing is going to go down, but it's no big deal."

First, always make sure that your ask is as reasonable and fair as can be. Ask yourself if you gave the other person enough lead time before asking them to meet your needs. Once you ascertain this, be direct about what you want.

These examples are like the 'starter pack" for manipulative behavior; they set the foundation for the rest of part 1 of this book. The chapters that follow will dissect some of the most prevalent manipulative behavior threads commonly practiced by the bulk of manipulative people. The most coercive people pretty much practice every one of them, while others may only predominantly lean on a couple of them to get their way.

The next chapter will cover these behaviors deeply and shed light on why these behaviors are coercive and harmful. Additionally, the chapter will seek to help you determine any of these behaviors.

Before we get into that, remember that the most manipulative behavior is guilt-tripping or using shame to manipulate others into giving in to your demands. The next chapter does a solid job of dissecting this:

Chapter 3: Do You Guilt-Trip or Make Others Feel Ashamed to Get Your Way?

Take a long, hard look at yourself and determine if you resort to making others feel guilty or ashamed to get your way. As you take a moment to consider this, keep in mind that it also involves engaging in typical childish behavior like pouting, whining, or crying.

Even if you often succeed in making others do your bidding by making them feel bad about themselves and undercutting their esteem, know that this is far from healthy behavior. Persisting with such behavior will only push people, even your loved ones, away from you over time.

A good way to look at it is this: any time you attempt to control or tug at someone's feelings for selfish reasons, that's manipulation at play. That's all there is to it!

Take an instance where you may say something to your partner along the lines of, "If you truly loved me, you'd stay home with me every night," "My friends are in shock that you treat me like this," or "I dislike it when we work on something together because I end up doing more than my fair share." The purpose of statements like these is to manipulate the other party into doing something for you.

Bringing up other things that they have done wrong, especially when such things do not relate to the immediate subject at hand, is another way manipulative people try to shame or guilt-trip people. Seasoned manipulators like to add in a dose of victim-play to bolster their guilt-tripping.

For instance, if you are trying to manipulate your partner into apologizing for irritability, you may say something like, "This is not the first time you've flown off the handle at me. Remember last week but one when I tried to explain something, and you said_____?"

You will play on others' feelings in an attempt to get them to do what you want. For example, you will make it known to your partner that what they did makes you deeply question how they feel about you. This will not be true in many cases, especially if the thing you are upset about is hardly serious. Either way, you will make the other person feel compelled to prove that they care about you by doing what you want.

Yet another way you may attempt to guilt-trip others is to remind them of the good things you have done for them. You will put their actions (or lack thereof) into stark contrast by making sure to bring up the good things that you have done for them—the grander or more recent the gesture, the better. Usually, you will gloss over the good things they have done for you as well as the bad things you may have done to them.

Speaking of bringing up prior good actions to coerce others into doing what they want them to do, manipulators love to use statements like, "after everything I have done for you/given you, how could you do this to me?" They will also say things like, "Well, I guess it meant nothing to you when I brought you those flowers the other day since you do not want to do what I'm asking you to," and "I have cooked dinner for you without fail yet you cannot remember to pick up a couple of milk packets on the way home."

That is extremely toxic behavior that just worsens things over time. Rather than appreciate your gifts or good deeds, people in your life will immediately start to wonder how long it will be before you use your gifts or good deeds as a stick with which to bludgeon them. That's why it is important to look at your life and see if you are prone to this behavior and others like them. If you are, then you are manipulative.

The next most common manipulative behavior is truth-twisting/lying to get what you want. The next chapter covers this aspect:

Chapter 4: Keeping Your Eye Peeled for Lying or Truth-Twisting

Keep your eye peeled for truth-twisting in your day-to-day interactions with others, which is essentially lying. Truth-twisting also involves intentionally misinterpreting something that someone else said or attempting to alter the context or meaning of something you said. In some instances, it may include withholding information to get your way.

For instance, you may say something like, "I am staying in tonight," and then later turn around and tell the person you are manipulating, "I meant we, you and I, would chill at home tonight."

Similarly, your colleague at work may have informed you that her portion of a joint project will likely be late due to a postponed meeting with a customer. You may persuade your employer to perceive you in a more favorable light by claiming, "I completed my task three days ago, but I am still pushing her to get her bit completed. It's even possible that I'll need to work on it myself."

Manipulators use truth-twisting as a means to "give themselves an out," thus preventing them from truly taking responsibility for things they said and, in the same stroke, pushing this responsibility they are neglecting from themselves and onto the other person. It's effectively a Swiss-army knife of sorts in the manipulator's arsenal.

Most of the time, manipulative people will pair truth-twisting with passive-aggressive, martyr-like behavior to make their coercion efforts more potent, much like they do when shaming or guilt-tripping others. Truth-twisting behavior is pretty much a weapon used to guilt-trip the opposite party more often than not.

For example, after saying, "I am staying in tonight," and later saying, "I meant both of us would be staying in tonight," a manipulative person will then add, "But it's alright, I'll just stay in and look up some vases on eBay on my own since you broke one last week."

By doing this, a manipulative person will make the other person feel bad, for something, in this case, for going out with a friend or coworker for an hour, despite the other person not having promised to stay in at any point during the day.

And if the other person confronts the manipulator by saying, "Well, why didn't you say outright that you wanted both of us to stay home tonight," the manipulator's reply will often be along the lines of, "But that's what I said! I don't have to break everything down to the last detail, do I? I mean, you're an adult, right?"

Look into your behavior, both at work/school and home, and determine if you engage in truth-twisting behaviors. As you examine your behavior, do not rationalize anything. If you engage in truth-twisting and even outright lying to get your way, you must own it. Be honest with yourself because, without this honesty, you will rationalize yourself into not working on yourself as a manipulator.

In the next chapter, we discuss another behavior very common with manipulators: withholding things—sex, money, emoting, etc.—to get your way.

Chapter 5: Telling if You've Been Withholding Things to Get Your Way

Notice if you've built a habit of withholding something if it means you will get your way. One of the easiest ways to manipulate somebody is to withhold something they want, such as aid, money, sex, or even love. This also includes withdrawing from them, stonewalling them, or refusing to engage in conversations with them.

At first, you may maintain control by withholding something from a person, but unfortunately, this control will be, at best, temporary. Eventually, the toxicity will drive the person away from you.

For instance, you may say something like, "Do not talk to me again unless you're giving me an apology," or "You can forget about me helping with the housework until you admit that you were in the wrong."

Besides shaming, guilt-tripping, and truth-twisting, the most common form of manipulation and abuse is withdrawing affection or acceptance. Many people will give you the cold shoulder and stonewall you if you turn them down and refuse to do something they want.

The primary reason why this tends to work so often is that it is our nature as human beings to seek approval. When people withhold acceptance or affection, it automatically hurts. After all, not a single person likes rejection. Rejection hurts even deeper if those rejecting you are people that you want to be with for whatever reason.

The most common way that couples wield this manipulation tactic is using intimacy and sex as a weapon, usually under the guise of "giving sex only when it is deserved."

However, this also happens with a lot of regularity in groups. You may have experienced this kind of avoidant abuse at school or even at work. If you have ever had the experience of having a group that made a point of leaving you out and maybe even made fun of you after isolating you, this was a perfect example of emotional withholding.

Cults utilize avoidant abuse to keep their followers in line. They understand that by instructing other followers to avoid contact with persons who have "sinned" or wish to quit the church or whatever kind of organization the cult is, those who leave would feel alienated, alone, and shunned. They stay put because they are afraid of rejection.

When a spouse does it, they often do it by staying in the relationship while intentionally refusing to be loving towards you, regardless of your pleadings. Attempts to reach out to them may result in a refusal to recognize your presence. When you attempt to make small talk at the dinner table, they'll be deafeningly quiet or only respond in singular words. Put simply, the person will make it clear that you are unimportant.

The worst thing about avoidant abuse is that the abuser(s) will frequently humiliate you or otherwise dismiss you if you express your qualms about their treatment of you. They will double down and make you feel like it is all your fault and that you'll have to work hard to earn their adoration once more. Think of it as a "dangling carrot" that you'll never succeed in snagging.

If you have done this, then you're most definitely manipulative and toxic.

Chapter 6: Playing the Blame Game as a Manipulation Maneuver

Manipulators are, at their core, disordered characters. And, perhaps, there is no behavior more common in disordered characters than the tendency to blame other people for their mistakes and shortcomings.

If you are manipulative, when someone confronts you about something you did that was hurtful, inappropriate, insensitive, or even harmful, you will immediately play the blame card. You will find a way to pin the blame on somebody or something else.

Most times, you will claim that the other individual or the circumstance forced you to do what you did rather than acknowledge that you indeed had a choice to do the right thing but instead failed to. You will play every card you can play to exempt yourself from responsibility.

Another name for the blaming tactic is "blame projection/projecting the blame." Projection, as a term, originates from psychodynamic psychology and alludes to one of the habitual mental actions classified as ego-defense mechanisms by conventional theorists.

The logic for this idea is that people often unintentionally "project" onto other people various reasons, intents, or behaviors that they harbor but are way too nervous or embarrassed to admit it.

Neurotic people indulge in projection mechanisms and defenses without even realizing it. As a manipulator, on the other hand, you are completely aware of your actions. Despite being completely at ease with your actions, you will be completely aware that your actions are wrong and viewed as wrong/immoral/hurtful, Etc. You just don't feel guilty or ashamed enough about your bad actions to commit to changing your ways.

It is more important to you that you "win the argument" and shift the blame away from yourself – thus allowing you to control the situation and other people– than it is to get to the bottom of the matter and ensure fairness all-round.

Blaming someone else for their wrongdoings is a manipulators' attempt to explain their situation by portraying themselves as being stuck in a predicament where they had no option but to do what they did. This way, they wriggle free from accountability while also manipulating and managing other peoples' perceptions. This strategy goes hand in hand with presenting oneself as a victim. It's a common way of getting people to focus on someone or something other than the manipulative person and their unlawful actions as the root of the problem.

Sometimes, this tactic of blaming is subtle. By drawing attention to a wide variety of contributing factors and circumstances, a manipulator may effectively obscure their role in the genesis of a problem. This "it isn't my fault" tactic is difficult to detect when your attention gets diverted to other "culprits" via this divertive sleight of hand.

Take a deep look into your life and see if you are prone to doing this. See if you shift the blame onto other people or circumstances and only take culpability when there is no wiggle room whatsoever. This behavior is common in people that have very low to no self-respect, but then again, so is the bulk of manipulative behaviors.

The next behavior common in manipulative people is vagueness, which we shall cover in the next chapter:

Chapter 7: Telling if You are Often Vague About What You Really Want

Take note if you are often vague about your desires. This could include dropping hints on what you would like done instead of communicating clearly and directly to the other person. Vagueness is, at its core, an unhealthy way of trying to get your wants and desires met. It is manipulative and betrays that you have minimal self-respect.

For instance, you will say, "I have nothing going on this Saturday," instead of directly asking your friend to accompany you to a movie.

As another example, let's say you're unhappy that some of your coworkers went out to lunch without you. A healthy way to handle this would be to talk to them directly to tell them that you're interested in going next time. However, as a manipulator, you could probably opt to gossiping about one of the people in attendance or finding a way of getting them into trouble, even for something completely unrelated.

Here's yet another example:

Let's assume that some of your acquaintances have organized a trip someplace and haven't invited you. Instead of asking them straight up why they didn't include you in their plans or telling them that you would like to go with them if that's fine with them, you mention how the car they are going in isn't all that suited to long road trips, thereby suggesting that your car is a better option. If this does not work, you move on to trash-talking where they are going, trying to diminish their experience before it even starts.

If you communicate vaguely, you shouldn't really expect specific results given that your communication is devoid of critical information.

Did you know that words account for less than 20% of communication? So, it makes sense to ensure that your words are clear!

How many times have you requested somebody to work on something for you, and then became enraged when they failed to do it exactly as you wanted it? Consider this: were you explicit in your description of how you wanted the job done, or did you leave hints in the hopes that the other party would catch the drift and execute accordingly? You won't get the task done properly if lean on hints to get your message through; it's likelier that you'll be waiting all day to no avail. Always keep in mind that different individuals perceive what you say in varied ways.

Sometimes, you might be imprecise and skim over things because you do not want to be crass and hurt others' feelings. However, if you want your relationships to truly develop and bloom, you must sometimes take chances and risk being blunt. But how?

Develop the ability to express and articulate yourself honestly and politely without getting bogged by the fear of upsetting others. Beyond this, instead of being ambiguous in the hopes of tugging at your opposite party's heartstrings so that they feel compelled to do your bidding, communicate your wishes and desires in a straightforward, succinct way. You may be wary of rejection – and the resulting hurt feelings – but being direct and honest will make sure there is no confusion about your position and will allow you to concentrate on other issues without wasting time. Furthermore, self-respecting persons are known for being direct and concise.

Chapter 8: The Drama Triangle—The Ultimate Manipulator's Tactic

Manipulative people – and narcissists – (though, in all honesty, manipulators tend to be narcissists and vice versa)— love to create havoc for other people, especially if it means that they get their way.

If you are manipulative, you will get a kick out of watching other people struggle, and rather than do everything you can do to stop the chaos, you will revel in the ruin going on around you and use it to make yourself feel superior. As a manipulative person, you will want to manipulate and control people to get your way and get a sense of supremacy, be it at school, at work, or in a romantic relationship.

You may not necessarily be conscious of this, but as a manipulative person, you dislike it when others get attention because you prefer to have the spotlight on you. How much attention you want on you will depend on the kind of manipulative person you are – closet, exhibitionist, or toxic. But in general, you will feel like you are winning – even when you are not – when the spotlight is on you.

The attention does not even have to be positive. All it needs to do is to keep your victims on their toes. You may do this by making up lies about the past and manipulating the person's present to ensure that they feel like they are going insane. You will also make a habit of switching between calmness and placidness to fierceness in seconds, quite like Jekyll and Hyde.

In the psychology world, there's a concept called the "drama triangle." It was created in the 1960s by Stephen Karpman. It outlines how individuals might play three distinct roles: victim, offender, and savior. If you are manipulative in any way, you will switch between these three personas fast and unexpectedly, leaving your victim with absolutely no idea of what to anticipate.

Perpetua Neo, a psychologist who also runs the 'Detox Your Heart' Program, says, "You are always walking on eggshells. You never truly know how to respond." If you are playing the victim and your (actual) victim responds with empathy – you will flip to persecutor seemingly on a switch. This way, you ensure that there is no way the other person can win. When you think about it, your victim isn't even playing, let alone playing to win, because you jumble everything and play by rules that heavily favor you.

One minute, everything will be going just fine – at least according to your victim – and then you will subject them to a bout of fierce, narcissistic rage. And your victim will neither see it coming nor respond properly. Rather than trusting their gut and knowing that they truly did nothing wrong, your victim will try and explain your manipulative, narcissistic behavior by blaming him or herself.

This often happens due to "love bombing," which happens at the start of the relationship. Love bombing is a manipulative tactic where you will suck in your target by showing them compliments, affection, and gifts, only to take all of it away. Your victim is then left wondering where they went wrong and automatically focuses the blame inward onto themselves.

Look out for the drama triangle in your life. Watch if you constantly flip from savior to persecutor to victim; from "I will go to bat for you" to "you are really stupid, completely worthless and nobody else will ever truly love you" to "how could you do this to me? How could you abandon me? You need to stop being so selfish and support me; otherwise, it will be your fault if I die."

It's important to note that out of all three components of this unsavory trifecta, the victim card will often be the most overplayed one. As a manipulative person, you will play this card significantly more than you do the other two. That is because you will, either consciously or unconsciously, know that it is necessary to frequently convince your victim(s) that you are the victim so that they automatically shift the blame onto themselves.

You will often use these victimhood behaviors, either by themselves or in combination – sad fishing, learned helplessness, and toxic empathy fishing.

Let's look at them individually:

> ***What is sad-fishing?*** This is when you make convoluted, exaggerated claims about your problems, emotional or otherwise, to generate sympathy. Sad-fishing, especially when a manipulator uses it, is a common reaction when they pretend to go through a hard time. As a manipulative person, you will use sad-fishing to tenderize your victim emotionally and thus manipulate and subject them to emotional abuse.

> ***Toxic empathy is*** when you over-identify with the other person's feelings and even directly take them as your own (or, in this case, pretend to take them as your own.) As a manipulative person, you will use this tactic to constantly keep your victim unbalanced, primarily via anxiety and "overcooking" the situation/circumstances at hand, thus having them perpetually ripe for emotional abuse.

> ➢ *Learned helplessness*, in the realm of psychology, is a mental state where an individual feels compelled to bear aversive stimuli or at least stimuli that are painful and unpleasant and becomes incapable or unwilling to avoid successive encounters with those stimuli – even when they are perfectly escapable – presumably because you have learned that you can't control the situation. As a manipulative person, you will pretty much be role-playing and using it to open up your victim for further manipulation and abuse.

With all this said, the drama triangle is a very toxic smoothie of verbal abuse, guilt-tripping, and what we can only describe as spasmodic affection. The human brain is programmed to primarily focus on the good and do its absolute best to blank out all the bad stuff. That means your victim (s) will explain away the toxic behavior like violence, shouting, and constant betrayal because of the times when you were sociable and affectionate toward them.

This mindset is one you need to break free from, and the chapters in the next part of the book will show you how to break out of this destructive behavior. They will arm you with the strategies – most of which will be overwhelmingly mental – to help you promptly recognize manipulative behavior in yourself (and in others) and nip it at the bud—mostly in yourself.

Part 2

Changing Manipulative Behavior

Chapter 9: Pave the Road for Change by Working on Your Self-Esteem

You may not know it, but the number one reason why people manipulate others is low self-esteem. This has stood true since the inception of man. A strong, confident man or woman with high self-esteem feels absolutely no need to manipulate others – it's just easier to win them over and hash something out; besides, it's less messy than manipulation and toxicity too.

If you feel somewhat unworthy of love or appreciation, then you will attempt to control and manipulate other people so you can keep them around. The idea – be it a conscious one or not – is that if you allow the other person to do as they please, they will eventually leave you for "better." The only way to have them around you is to manipulate and coerce them into staying.

You don't need deep introspection to figure out that this is not how healthy relationships function. The moment you feel the urge to manipulate and coerce, switch your attention to constructing/reconstructing your self-esteem. You will also find that bolstering your confidence will go a long way in improving your relationship.

Here are some ways that will instantly help you bolster your self-esteem and sense of self-worth:

⇨ Learn new skills

⇨ Work out consistently

⇨ Buy new outfits

⇨ Get a stylish haircut

Once you boost your self-esteem, you will automatically feel a decreased need to manipulate others. You will no longer worry about your partner or friends being with you because they feel obligated to – you will honestly believe that they are with you because they truly enjoy your company and think you are a cool, decent person.

Here are several strategies that you can use to boost your self-esteem:

#: *Make a concerted effort to be nice to yourself*

That tiny voice in your head that assures you that you are killing it (or not) is a lot more potent than you may realize. Make an effort to be nice to yourself, and if you happen to make a mistake, question negative thoughts and ideas that may follow. A decent rule of thumb is to talk to yourself as if you were talking to your friends. It may seem difficult at first, but practice really does make perfect.

#: *You do you*

Comparing yourself to others is a guaranteed way to make yourself feel bad about yourself. Rather than comparing yourself to others, focus on your objectives and accomplishments. The sort of pressure that comes with constantly comparing yourself with others is unnecessary.

#: *Move!*

Exercise increases motivation, helps you practice setting goals and helps build confidence and mental fortitude. Sweating also prompts your body to release endorphins – the 'feel-good' hormones.

#: *We all make mistakes – remember this*

Perfection is impossible (It's also boring too). Mistakes are a necessary part of the growth process. Do not beat yourself up if, say, you forget to hit CTRL+J on your final draft at work or school. Everyone has been there, even your seemingly perfect boss.

Chapter 10: Stop Yourself as Soon as You Notice Manipulative Behavior Kicking In

As soon as you notice manipulative behavior and habits creeping in, make every effort to stop yourself. Pause, take a step back and take a moment to reflect on the situation at hand and what you are doing. Take as long as you need to assess the situation and think about it – you do not have to tend to every situation immediately.

Talk to the other person – genuinely talk to them instead of just probing at the subject so you can find openings to impose your will on them – and get some perspective on how they feel.

Make it known to the person, without any vagueness, how you truly feel and why you think it would be better if they went about things the way you'd want them to. Be direct, honest, and above all, do not be vague.

One of the best ways to ensure that you are present in the situation and do not resort to manipulative behavior, even unconsciously, is to train yourself to respond instead of reacting.

Too many people – in fact, most people – move through life mostly reacting to people and situations. They rarely take the time to be introspective before offering their reply. Take your time to think and respond. Often, you'll only need a few seconds of thought to respond appropriately, and this will work far better for you than mindlessly reacting.

Remember that it is okay to take time on your own to figure your feelings out and work on them. The pressure to address everything ASAP is silly and unnecessary, especially when that pressure comes from you. It will also be hard to change your behavior.

Always give yourself time to take baby steps and progress slowly but steadily. You will not flip a switch and suddenly go from being manipulative to being completely non-manipulative. It will take time. Embrace this and be patient.

Most times, unless you are a psychopath, which you are certainly not, since you have the sense to seek this book out, you will not be intentionally manipulative. You will merely be repeating patterns and habits that you may have learned from your old relationships or even your family.

Here's something that will help you immensely if you apply it. If you are in the middle of talking to someone and recognize you are indulging in manipulative behavior, do not wait to finish whatever you were saying or want to explain yourself. Simply say, "I am so sorry to interrupt this conversation, but I really need a couple of minutes to think." You could also just excuse yourself and head to the bathroom for some privacy.

The next step related to this one is to learn how to listen to other people's perspectives on the situation with genuine interest.

Chapter 11: Listen to Other People's Perception on the Situation

Given all the talking that we do, you would think that we would be good at listening since there is no talking without listening. But in fact, research shows that we only recall between 25% and 50% of the things we hear. That means whenever you talk to your boss, your colleagues at work, your customers, or even your partner for ten minutes, they retain less than half of what you said to them.

The same is true for you too. When you receive directions or some information verbally, you do not hear the whole message either, or even the bulk of it. The hope is that the important bits are captured and retained in your 25-50%, but what if they are not?

Listening is very clearly a life skill that we all stand to benefit from honing. You will increase your productivity, in addition to your capacity to influence, convince, and negotiate, by improving your listening skills. You'll also prevent misunderstandings and conflicts. These are all important things, be it at work, school, your relationship, Etc.

Pay attention to the other individual's point of view on the matter at hand. You're probably just seeing things through your own eyes, which explains why you feel the need to manipulate to obtain your desires. Taking into account the feelings and sentiments of other people will assist you in overcoming these habits. Train yourself to allow others to express their thoughts and feelings without contemplating what you will say in return. Just let them have their moment. Then, find a middle ground that puts both of you in a winning position.

For instance, you may have plans to go out on Saturday night, while your spouse wants to spend the evening with colleagues from work. In that case, instead of guilting your spouse into dropping their plans for yours, please pay attention to how they feel about the issue. Then figure out how you will make it work so that everyone ends up happy. For example, you could reschedule your plans to go out on Friday night, thus allowing your spouse to spend time with colleagues.

It's okay if your spouse or partner cannot assist you in working through your manipulative behaviors; just ensure that you take full responsibility. It will be a bit self-defeating if you manipulate your partner into helping you eliminate your manipulative tendencies.

Active listening is a good technique to enhance your listening abilities. This is when you make concerted efforts to hear the words that someone else is speaking and the entire message delivered.

To truly do this, you need to really attention to the other person. You cannot let yourself get distracted by other things going on around you, even by your mind as it tries to construct counter-arguments while the other person is speaking. Even more so, you cannot allow yourself to get bored or drift off. Stay locked in. At first, it will be difficult, but the more you practice it, the easier it will become.

Chapter 12: Accept that You Cannot Reasonably Always Have Your Way

Perhaps more than anything, the ultimate eraser to manipulative behavior will be making the conscious decision to accept that you cannot always have things your way. And if you think about it, this is often the ultimate step in truly becoming a mature adult who's at peace with the world and its inhabitants.

Simply accept that you cannot always have things go your way. Granted, getting what you want will most likely make you feel good, but absolutely nobody gets what they want all the time. It's good to have a sober perspective on the real world: if you are always winning, then there is a 99% chance that those around you often feel compelled to forego and give up their desires to accommodate yours. That is nothing short of unfair. You need to be open and willing to compromise to establish true fairness in your relationships.

This is not to say that you should always seek to compromise. The world is inherently a selfish place, and even those closest to you will take advantage and diminish your desires if you're always tiptoeing when it comes to what you want.

If something is important to you, speak up and make it known that it is. This is okay. In fact, this is the right thing to do because it directly communicates your desires and intentions to others and also insures you from feeling resentful and bitter afterward.

Here's an example:

You may really want to get assigned a project that ultimately goes to another colleague at work. It is alright to feel disappointed – competitive people with a healthy ego and sense of self-worth will often desire the best pickings. But it is not healthy to make up lies about the person who got given the project in an attempt to undermine their reputation so that they get given the slim pickings next time. This may actually work in helping you get the next project, but overall, it will be negative, both for your reputation and career. It is also needlessly hurtful to the other person who is most likely just trying their best to put bread on their table and move their lives forward.

It's better to approach your manager in private and explain why you feel you deserve to work on a similar project in the future or at least a portion of it. Do this without diminishing the other person. You do not even have to mention them at all, except in passing. In fact, laud their abilities, and then make parallels to your own. This is how many people rise the corporate ladder without stockpiling enemies.

On a less competitive level, if you are off work on Thursday night and would like to go out but your partner wants to stay in, rather than playing on their emotions for not going along with what you want, order some takeout and watch some reruns together instead.

But all this will be easier to do once you consciously accept that you cannot always have your way. Doing so is the first step toward true freedom and peace of mind. It will also humble you and ground you in readiness for what the next chapter recommends: *take full responsibility for your feelings and needs.*

Chapter 13: Take Full Responsibility for Your Needs and Feelings

It would be best if you took full responsibility for your feelings and needs. You are the only one that can control your actions and reactions. Take time to ask yourself why you have certain feelings, then understand what you need to do to rectify your situation, especially if you engage in manipulative behavior that you want to break free from and change for good.

The truth is that at first, it will be hard to take full responsibility for your feelings. In fact, once you put yourself on the spot and force yourself to carry your own water emotionally, as opposed to saddling others with it, you will feel uncomfortable. However, it will be impossible to completely break free from toxic, manipulative behavior if you don't push yourself to face your emotions and take full responsibility for them. What is more, doing so is really empowering.

For instance, let us say that you are lonely and would like your friend or partner to come over, but they are busy with their own stuff. Rather than say something along the lines of, "Well, I guess you do not really care about me after all," to coerce them into dropping their things and coming over, you could take the initiative and do something engaging and fun by yourself. You could go see a movie or go shopping, Etc.

Once you train yourself to take responsibility for your emotions and your needs, you will, by default, eliminate the seeds that often prompt manipulative behavior in you. The other thing is that you will consciously force yourself to carry your load, emotional or otherwise, thereby greatly diminishing the need to manipulate others to do the carrying for you.

Here are some thoughts on how you can start taking on greater emotional responsibility:

> ***Make an objective or commitment*** that you reaffirm to yourself every day. Intentions are important. Day in day out, if you say things like, "Today, I will endeavor to embrace every facet of my life and take full accountability for my psychological, physical, emotional, and spiritual health and wellbeing," you will condition your brain to the point where it will begin to believe it. This practice takes mere minutes at most, and yet, it may have a significant influence on your interpersonal relationships.

➤ ***Talk with your spouse or partner***, or other people close to you, about your new way of living. Make it clear to them that moving forward, you would like to relate to them differently and that you would really appreciate their help in making it a reality. Ask them to let you know when you resort to manipulative, overbearing behavior rather than the "language of responsibility."

➤ ***Rehearse multiple times.*** Keep track of how your relationships progress. The proof is truly in the pudding (this is cliché, but it stands true nonetheless). You truly won't believe it until you experience how diverse conflict outcomes may very well be when things are just a little different. When someone is not on the defensive after being accused, little disagreements are easy to sort amicably instead of a terrible fight ensuing, resulting in wounded feelings. Pausing and being able to say things like, "I notice you're unhappy," or "I realize I'm annoyed and on edge," might help you (and others) identify emotional distress and empower you (and them) to go on and fix the situation. The process of conflict, acknowledgment, empathy and solution-finding is a lot smoother than the manipulative, overbearing elements of conflict, playing the blame game, stonewalling, and shutdown.

Once you take these steps, you will be well on your way to breaking free from manipulative and overall toxic behavior and relating to others on a more even keel.

But what if you attempt every suggestion in every chapter in this part of the book but still can't seem to make headway? The next chapter will suggest a fool-proof, last resort.

Chapter 14: The Importance of Working with a Counselor if All Else Doesn't Work

Changing behavior is considerably difficult, even in the most stoic, determined individuals. You may find that even after religiously following every directive in this book, you still struggle to purge manipulative, toxic behavior from your behavioral tendencies. If everything recommended up to this point fails, it's time to see a counselor or therapist.

Counselors are some of the best-placed people to help you identify behaviors that you need to change. Additionally, they will also explain the thought process behind your behavior and why it is necessary to adopt different ones. They will go even further and actively help you learn and adopt new healthier behaviors for you and those around you.

Psychologists study how individuals learn, evaluate experiences, and make their decisions through scientific research. They subsequently turn that information into strategies that work to assist individuals in making better decisions in their everyday lives.

Based on a deep well of knowledge on how lifestyles get influenced by multiple factors relative to mental processes, biology, and social relationships and interactions, a counselor will help you overcome the mental and emotional obstacles that prevent you from making smarter choices, like exercising regularly, working more efficiently, behaving in a mature, non-manipulative way, Etc.

A counselor will use the scientific study to help you tap into your potential and perform at an optimal level, mentally and emotionally. That will go a very long way in helping you break free from manipulative, toxic behavior.

Here are reasons why seeing a psychologist could help you break away from toxicity and coercive tendencies:

#: Psychology, at its core, is a social science

Psychology is a social science founded on proven methods and principles.

As such, nobody will be in a better position to help you be socially savvy as a psychologist will. The fact that a psychologist will approach the social aspect of living like a science means that they will explain why some behaviors are destructive, suggest new behaviors for you to substitute the old ones with, and show you how to go about adopting these new behaviors.

#: *Psychology will be a major help in understanding relationships*

The one thing any seasoned psychologist will tell you is that counseling does not automatically mean that everything will be perfect, or at least as it was before the issues started. But counseling will certainly arm you with better knowledge and comprehension of personal, familial, and even professional relationships.

You will understand that certain behaviors are toxic and harmful and how they affect those around you and what you can expect if you persist with them. This awareness will enable you to pinpoint and solve relationship problems that may not even relate to manipulative behavior long after the counseling, improving your life massively.

#: *Psychology will go a long way in building your critical thinking skills*

The information you absorb from your counselor or psychiatrist will help you understand your behaviors on a deeper level. It will also help you understand why they are inappropriate and what needs doing to supplant them. It will help you build your critical thinking skills since it will be founded on fact and, more importantly, logic.

Counseling will ultimately help you establish a grip on what will happen when some behavior or other precedes it. You will start to pause and think, "if I continue being a toxic human being to the ones I love, I may get my way and experience temporary fulfillment, but all this will loop back to me and harm me in the long run." You will steadily adopt the counselor's logical, methodical mindset after multiple counseling sessions. This element of improved critical thinking will spill over into other areas of your life and improve them greatly.

By this point in the book, you know what behaviors to look for and what to do to eliminate them and supplant them with new, positive ones. The next part of the book will explain how to build positive relationships as you work on your manipulative tendencies.

Part 3

Building Healthy Relationships

Chapter 15: Be Direct About What You Want Instead of Manipulating People

Anytime you lead a conversation, especially if you have a certain conclusion in mind and are seizing on some of the other person's comments while merely glossing over others, you are toeing the line between winning them over, or influence, and manipulation. Still, the line is there.

One of the best ways to distinguish it is to consider the outcomes every step of the way. Influence builds trust, likeability, and respect. Manipulation may (and often does) get results quicker, but the truth is that these results are often fleeting and built on shaky foundations.

Before long, the opposite party will build up resentment within themselves, which could prompt an explosive reaction from them down the line, or them taking their leave from you for good. Not only will you lose the company, respect, and love of someone that you are genuinely fond of, your reputation will likely take a massive hit.

Here is how you can exert influence, rather than resorting to manipulation:

⇨ ***Balance strengths and weaknesses in your engagements***

Everybody has both strengths and weaknesses. Manipulation, more often than not, zeroes in on weaknesses. Here's an example:

Let's say that you are trying to convince your coworkers to join you on weekend runs, and they happen to be middling and considerably unfit. You can push your suggestion onto them by explaining the vagaries of being unfit and overweight, such as being unable to indulge in certain activities or finding it difficult to attract romantic partners. In other words, you can shame them into buying into your idea, and this is inherently manipulative because you are homing in on their weaknesses (or, even worse, your misguided perception of them.)

A more influential approach wouldn't necessarily ignore the drawbacks of being unfit and overweight, but it would balance them out with the perks of improved physical fitness. Rather than dwell on tired stereotypes about folks with 'rounder' body types, you would mostly emphasize the perks of adopting an active lifestyle.

It's also important to consider who wins when you have conversations like this one. Influence is all about having a win/win scenario. On the other hand, manipulation only has you winning, and you couldn't care less whether the other person wins or not: "we both get something we want" versus "I get my way at the other person's expense."

⇨ *Does it feel "icky"?*

Sure enough, icky is not the most scientific term but always trust your gut. If something does not feel right, the chances are high that it isn't. Tweak your approach to ensure that you error on the side of influence whenever you make a mistake. After all, there is no such thing as being "only a little manipulative:" you are either manipulative towards someone or not.

⇨ *The element of choice is important*

Does the other person really have a choice? And can she see that she actually has one? Manipulation often has a "this is the only option" stance. You will make the other person feel and believe that success is impossible if they do not do things your way. Make sure that in your engagements with others, you actively position yourself, or your idea, as just one of the choices on the table.

Focusing on building influence is the first step to take. The next step is to train yourself to be comfortable with getting 'no' for an answer.

Chapter 16: Learn to Accept 'No' for an Answer Without Guilting or Shaming Others

You may want to draw up plans with somebody or perhaps want a favor. In some cases, they may say 'no' to you. When you get a no, please take a deep breath and let it go. The other option is often manipulation, where you try to shame the person into doing things your way.

Let us say you want your younger sister to watch your kids because you want to go out. If she declines and tells you she has plans, thank her for being someone you could reach out to and look at other alternatives. Do not respond with, "Well, I guess you do not like spending time with your nephews and nieces after all."

Similarly, you may want your boss to allow you a day off work, but your boss tells you that can't happen. They may even give you a valid reason, such as the week being an especially busy one. Do not moan and say things like, "I knew you'd say 'no.' I mean, I am the only person you never allow to have off days."

It does not matter who you are, where you work, what you've seen, where you've been, et al. It will never get easier getting "no" for an answer, no matter how many times you hear it. Some of the most prominent businessmen the world has ever seen admit to being stung when they faced negative answers. However, many of them have learned that a no maybe a simple redirection onto better things. Adopt a similar mindset, and you will find that suddenly, you do not feel compelled to undercut others to have them do your bidding.

In your career and life as a whole, you will run into non-affirmative answers all the time. Some people will courteously follow up with valid reasons, while others will say no and leave it at that. For example, your employees, if you run a business, may turn you down. It is necessary to learn to cope with being faced with "no" answers. Learn to recalibrate quickly. In fact, the more successful you become and the more people you meet, the more 'no' answers you will get.

It is vital to learn just how to respond to a no and recalibrate accordingly. Of course, just like with most strategies in this book, doing this not as easy as it sounds. But with enough practice, it will eventually become second nature.

Once you have this down pat, the next step is to learn how to respect the boundaries of others.

Chapter 17: Learn to Respect Other Peoples' Boundaries

Manipulators often have a poor sense of personal boundaries. That's why you need to learn to allow other people to enjoy their personal space and respect the decisions they make for themselves. Along the same lines, do not try to change people.

For example, do not insist on calling a person if they have expressed to you that they want a break. If you are unhappy with some behaviors that your partner has adopted recently and find yourself feeling ever more resentful, talk to your partner and see if you can arrive at a compromise. Under no circumstance is it okay to try to manipulate your partner into fitting into your preconceived notion of an ideal partner.

For instance, you may want your partner to shed off a few pounds so that she looks like she did when you first met. Rather than say, "Wow darling, you look like you're auditioning for the role of Jabba the Hutt lately," which is manipulative, not to mention mean, see if you can influence them into indulging in fitness activities that will help them lose weight. Chapter 15 covered how to influence others instead of manipulating them.

Here are some tips that will help you respect other people's boundaries:

#: *Communicate clearly and ask questions*

We covered vagueness and the importance of communicating clearly and directly. Clear communication is vital to understanding a person's boundaries are.

Always pay close attention to how other people respond in conversations and their body language. Do they appear comfortable? Do they give the appearance of a person who is closed off? Are they dropping hints that they'd like to end the conversation, or at least divert it elsewhere?

If you are not sure, don't be afraid to ask questions. Give them the option of establishing their boundaries. This way, you will know whether or not you are encroaching.

#: *Accept what the other person communicates*

Accepting what somebody else is saying as valid can be especially difficult if you are not used to it or have been a manipulative person for a long time.

The boundary the other person is putting up may make little to no sense to you. It may even look silly. However, it still is their boundary, and as such, worth respecting.

If you feel you really can't or do not want to, it may be a smart choice to move away from the person or perhaps focus on someone else whose boundaries are more in line with your expectations.

Here's an example:

Let's say you grew up in a lively household where banter, roasting, and ribbing were normal. Your family would lightly pick on each other all the time as a sign of respect and affection, but never in a mean-spirited way. However, your romantic interest or spouse grew up in a more 'somber' household where ribbing was not common at all. In this case, your partner may take offense when you banter or roast them. They may even get angry.

Rather than try to manipulate and guilt them into accepting your banter by pointing out how excessively sensitive they are, dig a little deeper and see why they dislike banter and allow them to live as they want to. Missing out on a bit of banter won't kill you after all.

#: Respect other people's autonomy

Manipulative people often overstep boundaries because they think they know better and can make better decisions for the other person. You may have a genuine desire to help and protect but resort to stepping on the other individual's boundaries to accomplish this.

Other than obviously violating the other person's boundaries, the other main issue with this kind of approach is that it keeps them from developing useful skills and valuable experiences that they need to lead their lives optimally.

Take a step back and allow them the opportunity to make the mistakes they need to make (if necessary) to learn from them and have better experiences in the future.

Chapter 18: Do Nice Things Without Necessarily Expecting Anything in Return

Train yourself to do nice things for others without necessarily expecting anything back. It is amazing when people respond to your kindness by doing nice things in return. However, expecting people to behave a certain way when you do nice things for them is manipulative. Learn to adopt a "no strings attached" stance when you do nice things to others.

For example, let's say you bought a Starbucks latte for your coworker. Do not expect them to do the same for you the next time they are out.

Here's another example; you may offer to watch another person's kids while they're away dealing with some situation or other. Do not expect the person to pay you for your service or get you a gift—unless they insist on it or offered to do it in advance.

The most important gift anyone can give you is time. We live in a world where everyone is seemingly busy, and people will throw every excuse in the book at you to explain why they cannot see you. Now, the people who really want to see you will make time for it. But if they can't, don't take it too much to heart. Let it slide and focus on yourself.

Here is something else you'll discover very quickly: giving people things without expecting anything in return very often turns into something amazing. Some people call it karma, and maybe that's just what it is. But we are in a world that is extremely fast-moving, where we expect prompt responses. However, this is not really how the universe works. This is not to say that there is anything wrong with expecting prompt replies and responses, but when it comes to giving, the return, more often than not, comes much later.

The other thing is that you should not be afraid to ask for help, particularly when it comes to people you have gone out of your way to assist in the past. You will be surprised at just what people are willing to say yes to when asked properly. And most 'no' answers will rarely be outright 'no's,' but rather, "not right now, but I can make it work later,' or something along those lines. As such, when you get declined, try later, and maybe the 'no' will have changed to a 'yes.'

The key point here is that you will do more than foster glowing relationships with those around you when you train yourself to give without expecting anything back. You will also help erase manipulation from your side, but it will also often sow seeds that you will get to reap in the future.

Conclusion

By now, you've pretty much learned everything you need to learn to unearth and then break your manipulative ways. It will take a great deal of hard work, alertness, and consistency to experience true, tangible change.

But if you implement the strategies in this book, you have a solid foundation to overhaul your ways and become a better husband/spouse, workmate, colleague, friend, boss, Etc.

You'll likely slip many times, but you must get up immediately, dust yourself off, and keep moving. That is the way to engineer true change, especially when it comes to habits since these are often hard to break. But once you get rid of your manipulative ways, you will be so much happier for it, and every relationship in your life will improve vastly.

PS: I'd like your feedback. If you are happy with this book, please leave a review on Amazon.

Please leave a review for this book on Amazon by visiting the page below:

https://amzn.to/2VMR5qr